Poems

Published in 2013 by
Liberties Press
140 Terenure Road North | Terenure | Dublin 6W
Tel: +353 (1) 405 5703
www.libertiespress.com | info@libertiespress.com

Trade enquiries to Gill & Macmillan Distribution
Hume Avenue | Park West | Dublin 12
T: +353 (1) 500 9534 | F: +353 (1) 500 9595 | E: sales@gillmacmillan.ie

Distributed in the UK by
Turnaround Publisher Services
Unit 3 | Olympia Trading Estate | Coburg Road | London N22 6TZ
T: +44 (0) 20 8829 3000 | E: orders@turnaround-uk.com

Distributed in the United States by
Dufour Editions | PO Box 7 | Chester Springs | Pennsylvania | 19425

ISBN: 978-1-907593-66-6
2 4 6 8 10 9 7 5 3 1
A CIP record for this title is available from the British Library.

Cover design by Fergal Condon | fergalcondon@gmail.com
Internal design by Liberties Press
Printed by Bell & Bain Ltd

The publishers gratefully acknowledge
financial assistance from the Arts Council.

Poems

Sheila Wingfield

Selected, edited and introduced by

Lucy Collins

With a foreword by Brendan Kennelly

LIB
ERT
IES

Contents

Acknowledgements

I would like to thank the following institutions for permitting me to use their resources: the Trustees of the National Library of Ireland; the Board of Trinity College Dublin Library; and the Board of University College Dublin Library. Members of staff at these libraries have been very helpful to me during the period I was working on this book.

Thanks to Hon. Lady Langrishe and to David Pryce-Jones for permission to print these poems; and to Brendan Kennelly, the Irish Newspaper Archive and the *Sunday Independent* for allowing me to reprint the Wingfield review in full. I am grateful to many people for encouragement, as well as practical advice, in the course of preparing this volume: Andrew Carpenter, Alex Davis, Gerald Dawe, Anne Fogarty, Margaret Kelleher, Anne Mulhall and Jody Allen Randolph. I am especially grateful to Philip and Patsy Harvey for their support and guidance throughout. I would also to thank Seán O'Keeffe, Daniel Bolger, Alice Dawson and the rest of the team at Liberties Press for their commitment to this project.

.

Lady, I Bow to Your Diversity[1]

Sheila Wingfield has this to say about her own poetry:

> As for subject-matter – the Irish and English coun-
> tryside and country ways in general are so deeply
> rooted in me that I fancy much of this blows
> through my work. History, archaeology, folklore
> and the superb economy of the classical Greeks are
> other influences. These tendencies came together
> in forming my poetic outlook. This can be stated
> simply. What is personally felt must be fused with
> what is being, and has been, felt by others. But
> always in terms of the factual. Nothing woolly or
> disembodied will do.

The strong simplicity of that statement is typical of a writer
who knows what she wants to say and also how to say it. Her
poetry is almost unfailingly fresh and direct. This three-line
poem, entitled 'Winter', from *Poems* (1938) is typical not just of
her early poems but of her entire work.

> The tree still bends over the lake,
> And I try to recall our love,
> Our love which had a thousand leaves.

The distinguished poet and critic, Sir Herbert Read, said of
her long poem *Beat Drum, Beat Heart* that it was 'the most sus-
tained meditation on war that has been written in our time'.
This poem, in four powerful parts, is by turns calm and savage,
contemplative and explosively dramatic. Her use of soldiers'
voices, like cries from the depths of hell, is harrowingly effective.

'I was a Greek. I climbed Aornos' rock for Alexander.
My foot slipped on the pine needles and my breath
    hurt.
Round me men hurtled down to where the Indus
Washes that great crag.'

> O men O commanders

'I lived by the Border. Mist would bead our woollen
    cloaks,
Our pelts and faces, on the mornings when we woke
Ready for foraying. I died in the grass
As lonely as a crow.'

I think that Sheila Wingfield's main strength as a poet is that she can go from a long meditative work, such as *Beat Drum, Beat Heart*, which deals with whole cultures and peoples and histories, to brief poems which, because they are vividly presented pictures, are quite haunting. A good example is 'A Bird':

> Unexplained
> In the salt meadow
> Lay the dead bird.
> The wind
> Was fluttering its wings

Sheila Wingfield excels at expressing quiet, even reticent, emotions. Her melancholy affection for Dublin is, for this reason, all the more memorable.

> Part elegant and partly slum,
> Skies cleaned by rain,
> Plum-blue hills for a background;
> Dublin, of course.
> The only city that has lodged
> Sadly in my bones.

These two books (*Her Storms* and *Admissions*) are the work of a poet of unusual gentleness, strength and emotional depth.

Whether writing of a Dublin museum or an Italian villa, of Romney Marsh or a small Irish town, her poetry is always lucid, precise and musical. At times, she reaches genuine sublimity, as in 'Blinded Bird Singing'. And her tribute to Saint Brigid is a delightful blend of pleasant irony and generous homage:

> Brigid, once
> Protector of poets;
>
> Patron of Kildare
> Where nowadays foxhounds
>
> Keep muzzles down to the scent
> While bullocks fatten;
>
> Worshipped by Romans
> Under Severus in York;
>
> Protector from domestic fires
> In Ireland
> And now its own saint;
>
> Lady, I bow to your diversity.

Reading through these books, one is compelled to say to Sheila Wingfield what she herself says to Saint Brigid:

> Lady, I bow to your diversity.

Brendan Kennelly
Dublin, 1977

---

[1] Originally published as a review of *Her Storms* (Dolmen Press, 1977) and *Admissions* (Dolmen Press, 1977), *Sunday Independent*, December 25, 1977.

'Just What We Are': The Poetry of Sheila Wingfield

I

'If only I could "sing like a bird on a bough"' wrote Sheila Wingfield in 1954, as she reflected on the challenges of a poet's life. 'As a writer, I am tentative, laborious and immensely slow ... Work is least hard early in the morning, on waking, when the critical senses seem washed and clear; but at best it is an arduous affair'. Everywhere in her reflections on her writing we find evidence of her painstaking approach to the process and of the combined pleasure, grief and tension that it yielded. Difficult though this commitment may have been for Wingfield personally, it produced work of extraordinary depth and clarity; intellectually suggestive with a mood of combined restraint and intensity. Varieties of form, of image and sound pattern, testify to the poet's linguistic energies; yet at the centre of each poem lies a stillness that is as mysterious as it is critically demanding. Rarely autobiographical, Wingfield's art is shaped from the very constraint she experienced creatively, and thus remains caught in an intense and difficult process of self-realisation.

Wingfield found it hard to identify exactly how an individual poem emerged. In a commentary for the Poetry Book Society in 1954, she reflected on the complexity of her craft: for her, form and theme came together as an indissoluble unit; she returned to lines and phrases already composed, and formulated new ones as she sought to shape these into a whole. Her description of the method indicates its sensitivity, and suggests how difficult it was to predict the course that such inspiration might take. Yet it also construes composition as a continuous process, and one that profoundly shapes the poet's interaction with the world. For Wingfield it was as though all language was seen from the perspective of the poetic line, all thoughts brought to bear on existing creative preoccupations. Her poems are complex works, both intellectually and emotionally, though they do not always advertise their depth of learning, and hardly ever their depth of feeling. Kathleen Raine described Wingfield as 'a true poet with that intelligence of feeling that is woman's authentic contribution to knowledge', but Wingfield's gender, as well as her class, would prove an impediment to her literary career, and especially to her standing among twentieth-century Irish poets. Its reticence is one of the reasons why her work has been neglected, yet paradoxically it is what makes her poetry still fresh and intriguing today. The disciplined mood of her poetry does not estrange, rather it moves us, because of its unflinching attention to the details of human experience. In her prose too, Wingfield reflected carefully on the forces in her life that made her what she was; yet these are mediated through the perspective of a reader and thinker, a testament to the breadth of her enquiry into philosophical and aesthetic concerns.

The range and intensity of Wingfield's engagement with issues of thought and language developed early. Born in England of an Irish mother and an Anglo-Jewish father, Sheila Beddington – as she was then known – had a privileged upbringing that combined the sophistication of London life with the freedom of summers spent with her grandparents at Bellair in County Offaly. From the beginning, though, this was a life of doubleness: her father's Jewish heritage was suppressed in favour of assimilation into British upper-class culture; her Irish identity subordinated to the social demands of her upbringing. As Penny Perrick's absorbing biography of Wingfield has shown, self-division would be an enduring trait both in the poet's life and work. Sheila's childhood love of reading instilled in her a near-endless desire to be immersed in other worlds, both imagined and real. It also contributed to her awareness of the important continuities inherent in the literary process; the traditions that shape every reader, the private patterns that can be traced between one text and another. Her relationship with her mother was a difficult one, and books became a retreat from humiliating exchanges as well as a shared interest with her older brother, Guy. Sheila was deeply attached to her father, and though they had a warm bond, Claude Beddington disapproved of his daughter's literary interests, perhaps because he feared they would make her less attractive to eligible men. This response taught the poet another, more painful, lesson: that it might be impossible to reconcile her desire for a literary life with the larger social pressures to which she would be subjected once grown to adulthood.

Educated at Roedean and later sent, not to university, but to a French finishing school, Sheila Beddington was being groomed for marriage into the British upper classes. It was at this time that she suffered the first, and greatest, loss of her young life, when in 1925 her brother Guy died from tuberculosis while undergoing treatment at a sanatorium in Munich. When her parents' marriage ended, not long after Guy's death, Sheila chose to remain in her father's household, hosting his parties and accompanying him to social and sporting events. It was at one such event – a hunt in Ireland in the spring of 1932 – that she met her future husband. Pat Wingfield was the heir to the Powerscourt estate in County Wicklow, once one of the largest estates, and finest houses, in Ireland. A series of Irish Land Acts from 1870 had culminated in the major redistribution of estates following the establishment of the Irish Free State in 1922, and by the time Pat Wingfield met his bride-to-be the future of the entire Powerscourt estate was in doubt. Beddington money would play a vital role in allowing the traditions of Powerscourt to continue, and in her choice of husband Sheila accepted a position in Ireland's dwindling Ascendency class, choosing status over creative freedom. The tension between these would remain, however, and often became unbearable in the years to come. It would leave Wingfield unable to fulfil either the role of the hostess or that of the artist with ease, and created lasting feelings of dissatisfaction that contributed to her frail health and exerted a destructive force on almost all her relationships.

The Wingfield's marriage was happy at first, and unlike many of her female precursors, Sheila Wingfield found that she had more time to read and write as a married woman than she had while living at her father's house. In spite of this, tensions between domestic and artistic roles re-emerged. Likewise, divisions between the desire for recognition as a poet, and a love of privacy – even secrecy – shaped Wingfield's art in important ways. Living first in Kent, with regular visits to Ireland, Wingfield was eager for literary connections on both sides of the Irish Sea. In Dublin, her friendship with Francis Hackett and his wife Signe Toksvig opened doors to the *Dublin Magazine*, where she published regularly during the 1930s. The *London Mercury* also accepted early work. She became a close friend of Ottoline Morrell in the last year of Morrell's life and relished the access to other writers and artists that this connection made possible. Through her, Wingfield met John Hayward who, as literary advisor to the Cresset Press in London, was instrumental in having her first manuscript placed there. Though the prospect of a major publication, with all the visibility that this entailed, caused Wingfield some apprehension – especially concerning her family's response – she was ambitious for literary success. Her unguarded use, in the promotion of this first book, of some private words of encouragement that W. B. Yeats had written to her, provoked outrage in the Nobel Laureate. The dispute left Wingfield chastened but no less anxious to record the responses of poets and critics to her work. From this point onward she was acutely conscious of her reception as a poet; her archive contains albums in which are pasted the printed reviews of all her publications. These are meticulously annotated in Wingfield's distinctive handwriting; errors of fact are corrected and unfriendly critics reproved. Yet in 1965 when an interviewer asked her what audience she had in mind for her work, she replied 'absolutely none, it's a private affair'. These contradictions, which highlight the divided self that shaped Wingfield's poetic persona so powerfully, also made it difficult for her to achieve creative satisfaction, since her aims as a writer remained unclear, even to herself. Acknowledging a feeling of satisfaction once a work was completed, Wingfield claimed that she was later too embarrassed even to open one of her own books. In fact, she studied her own published volumes carefully, noting the smallest of errors and suggesting revisions for later editions. More significantly, many of her poems were substantially revised between original publication and her *Collected Poems* of 1983, indicating her continuous engagement with her own creative process. From her first publication to her last, Wingfield's tireless questioning is everywhere evident, both in her approach to the dissemination of her work, and in the major themes of her poetry.

Though Wingfield's predicament had some unique circumstances, it is in some ways indicative of the place of the Irish woman poet at this time. Though women had played a major role in political and cultural events in Ireland before the 1916 Rising, they were quickly marginalised once national and party political concerns began to dominate public discourse during the early Free State years. This situation was in fact part of a much larger reduction in cultural activity: the 1930s, when Wingfield first began to publish, was a low point in Irish literary history. The Censorship of Publications Act had been passed in 1929, and though few poets had their work banned, the atmosphere of the time had a depressive effect on literary innovation, and caused many writers to leave Ireland altogether. Publishing opportunities were also scarce, and key periodicals were often identified with close-knit groups of contributors. For poets, two journals were of particular consequence in the early decades of Wingfield's career: the *Dublin Magazine* had begun publication in 1923 and survived, with some editorial variations, until 1958. Its longevity, rare in journals of this time in any part of the British Isles, was partly due to its reputation for conservatism. In contrast to *The Bell*, which would first appear in 1940, it never sought to challenge the status quo. In spite of this, the *Dublin Magazine* was surprisingly generous in its inclusion of women – more than sixteen women poets were counted among its contributors and their work included translations, sonnet sequences and long poems. Wingfield was a significant presence there during the 1930s, when literary styles varied between late Revivalism and modernist experimentalism. For the most part, though, she placed individual poems with British periodicals and newspapers, including the *London Magazine*, the *New Statesman* and the *Times Literary Supplement*. Irish journals, such as *Poetry Ireland*, would help to shape the Irish poetry scene from the 1950s onward, but by the time this renaissance was under way, Wingfield had already begun to distance herself from Ireland and would spend much of her remaining time abroad.

Though Ireland's journal culture was by no means moribund during Wingfield's writing years, its publishing industry was remarkably weak. Following the closure of Maunsel in 1926, most Irish poets turned to England to find publishers for their work and for Wingfield this was a natural choice, given that she had been raised there, and it continued as her main residence until shortly after the outbreak of the Second World War. Wingfield published with the Cresset Press in London until the 1960s, when she brought out one volume – *The Leaves Darken* – with Weidenfeld and Nicholson in 1964 before moving to the Dolmen Press. Dolmen would publish two titles by her, *Her Storms* and *Admissions*, both of which appeared in 1977 and were subsidised by Wingfield. Liam Miller, who ran Dolmen Press, and Wingfield herself hoped the move to an Irish publisher would renew interest in her work that had waned considerably for more than a decade, but in spite of strong reviews this aim remained largely unrealised.

There were interesting thematic and stylistic developments in poetry by Irish women during this time, though Wingfield was only partly in tune with these changes. Much work by women showed an increasing concern with the inner life, and with creative processes, perhaps reflecting a shift away from political and social preoccupations in the earlier decades of the century. It was a pattern that reflected the pre-eminence of subjective experiences in art and literature internationally and would remain an important dimension in poetry even through periods of postmodern predominance. In this respect it is particularly significant that so few of the women who came to prominence in either the British or Irish poetry scenes during the 1930s and 1940s would be acknowledged by the next generation of women writers. This is particularly noteworthy in the Irish context, where mid-century poets such as Wingfield, Rhoda Coghill, Mary Devenport O'Neill and Blanaid Salkeld were all but erased from the history of Irish poetry. Eavan Boland, herself a poet of the later generation, has written about a meeting she had with an elderly Wingfield, and her description may go some way to explaining this seeming disavowal: 'I must have told her that I was a poet. And yet there was nothing mutual or properly engaging in my attitude. In my secret mind I shrank from her talk of disappointment. I could make no sense of her harsh retrospective on loss and exclusion.' The next generation looked to the future, not to the troubled past.

II

As Wingfield later remembered it, 'Odysseus Dying' was the first poem she wrote. If this is true it is remarkable for its taut realisation of intense yet understated emotion, all the more so since it drew inspiration from the early death of the poet's brother, Guy. The poem combines two characteristics that would be important as Wingfield's writing developed: the attentive use of classical materials and the unflinching scrutiny of states of human transition. The clear yet equivocal opening 'I think Odysseus, as he dies, forgets/Which was Calypso, which Penelope' at once calls attention to the voice of the individual speaker yet allows that speaker to fade from view as the poem progresses. Much of Wingfield's work is similarly reticent; she desires always to explore but never to reveal the self fully, a strategy she clarified in these terms: 'What is personally felt must be fused with what is being, and has been, felt by others.'

Her attraction to the most concise of poetic forms is testament to her lightness of touch. The three-line 'Winter' with its simple natural imagery turns on the speaker's suspension between the emotional stillness of the present and the apparent boundlessness of past love. Its containment is expressive even as it resists any form of extended revelation.

The sense of being between states inflects Wingfield's entire first collection. This is perhaps unsurprising, as the transition to the public role of poet that Wingfield experienced with the appearance of *Poems* (1938) was both exhilarating and troubling for her. The sanction, whether real or imagined, that her father and then her husband seemed to place on her participation in literary life created an almost unbearable tension which resulted in the poet succumbing to an unspecified illness at this time, a pattern that would repeat itself whenever the contest between the different elements of her life grew too great. 'The Change' evokes the emotional implications of such transitions: its depiction of memorable sensory experience, and the syntactical skill with which inner transformation is rendered, is important to this poem's theme of emergence from an intense experience of love. It is also essential to the movement between states of dream and reality, as the poem 'The London Square' suggests.

These early poems reveal some key features of Wingfield's formal achievement too: her use of a range of poetic models, from fixed forms – such as the sonnet – to free verse; her combination of tonal complexity and syntactical clarity, even within a single short poem. In this respect, Wingfield is the inheritor of a modernist sensibility, though her work does not exhibit the fragmentation of form or radical linguistic shifts that are often associated with the modernist movement. She invokes a cosmopolitan sensibility here – another hallmark of the modern – showing herself to be open to a range of cultural influences, both thematically and formally. She cannot be seen, either at this time or later, as a distinctively 'Irish' poet, in the narrow sense. In spite of this, her poems show human experience to be shaped by place, and Wingfield, who would later affirm its importance in her creative life, evokes both sensory environments and specific geographical locations with flair. This is equally true of her treatment of historical and contemporary settings. Her interest in ancient history, especially that of the East, is evident from her earliest work, yet her attention to contextual detail is not driven solely by aesthetic concerns, but by the need to engage with the circumstances of character and action. In spite of the controlled energies of Wingfield's work during the 1930s, there is a haunted quality to her landscapes; they are marked by death and difficult emotional transitions. From the fate of the king in 'Chosroe the Second' to the ghosts of 'barrack square' and 'tenement' in 'The Dead', these poems invoke both human transience and the personal difficulties of Wingfield's early life.

Poems (1938) was well received by critics, so it is strange that for her second volume – *Beat Drum, Beat Heart* (1946) – Wingfield should depart so radically from the form of this early work. Her creative transition was partly shaped by the changes in Wingfield's family life brought about by the Second World War. Her husband was a captain in the 8th Huzzars; captured in Libya, he would spend more than three years in an Italian prisoner of war camp. Sheila, for her part, was dispatched to Bermuda. Her father was anxious about the fate of Jews in Europe and wanted to be sure that his only remaining child would be safe from harm. The separation took its toll on the Wingfield marriage, and the immediacy of war opened a new vein of exploration in her poetry. At the time of its publication, Herbert Read called *Beat Drum, Beat Heart* 'the most sustained meditation on war that has been written in our time', but critic Alex Davis is right to judge the sequence as exceeding the theme of war. The title of the poem itself suggests a public/private binary, and its form indicates both the separate and contingent roles that still mark relationships between the sexes – the strongest indication of this being the title of its four parts. Though Wingfield denied seeing herself as a feminist, it is in this poem that she records most directly the importance of acknowledging the fullest extent of women's intellectual and emotional character.

In the first part of the poem, 'Men in War', the strain and confusion of conflict is foremost; the darkness in which the soldiers labour is both a physical state and an existential condition. In this darkness the self is obliterated: 'And now not I, but at all cost/The other must be saved from harm'. The voice in this section of the poem is at times singular, at times collective, and it is significant that Wingfield imputes the same perspective to soldiers from the Spanish Civil War and those from the Eastern Front during the Second World War. In all cases the physical pressures and emotional turmoil irrevocably alter the soldiers' sense of individual identity and challenge lyric assumptions concerning the singular coherent subject in the poem. Even in the second part of *Beat Drum, Beat Heart*, which is set in peacetime, the question of how the individual subject can relate to the wider world remains. Though differentiated, these figures now move in a mutable world where finding one's bearings is challenging, and linguistic and visual signifiers such as texts and maps proliferate, rather than clarify, meaning.

In contrast to these feelings, the second half of *Beat Drum, Beat Heart* – that voiced by woman – is frequently concerned with empowerment and instinctive knowledge. Instead of being obstructed or unclear, actions are smooth. 'How easy to move, to act!' declares the speaker in 'Women in Love', where the pattern of alternately indented lines suggests a flow of energy pulsing through the poem. The power here, which is both linguistic and psychological, is not grasped but held freely, and is further realised in the final section of the poem as the woman's sense of renewal unites tradition and innovation through an almost Yeatsian faith in the powerful energies of opposition. The poem as a whole, though multi-vocal, has a strong Irish dimension, and heralds a more distinct sense of place in Wingfield's developing work.

A marker of this shift is laid down early in the poet's next volume, *A Cloud Across the Sun*, published three years later in 1949. Here 'Ireland' reinforces Wingfield's connection to the country after a long period away from it; yet this connection is defined by opposition – it is 'the country/That has no desolation, no empty feel'. In Wingfield's reading, Ireland's ancient past is ever-present but the quietness of the scene does not succeed in making it wholly peaceful. It is interesting to set this poem alongside others with the same title by Wingfield's precursors. Poems, each also titled 'Ireland', by Susan Mitchell (1906) and Dora Sigerson Shorter (1907) display variations on the allegorical mode; Wingfield's poem is unique in the subtlety of its response, however, and in the quietness of diction that belies complex and troubled feelings. 'Ross Abbey', from the same collection, enacts a similar tension, though the path it takes is more conventionally poetic, evoking Wordsworth in its direct address to a place beloved in childhood, and couched in those romantic terms. Yet at its close the poem seems to record the failure of such romanticism: '[u]ntil that middle-aged, that rainy day/I saw you once again, then looked away'.

Much of Wingfield's work records such resistance to easy consolation, as the fine 'Poisoned in Search of the Medicine of Immortality' concludes – 'To be at rest/Is but a dog that sighs and settles: better/The unrelenting day'. So it is appropriate that her poems increasingly turn away from familiar scenes and connections towards deeper exploration of the human condition. We begin to see her use of Classical materials not as an imaginative escape from contemporary realities, but as a way of exploring the continuities in humanity's quest for meaning. Alex Davis has spoken of Wingfield's search for archetypal emotions from this source, and she also uses it as a way of engaging with aesthetic and philosophical issues, giving them visual and imaginative weight. 'Sectio Divina' explores the concept of the 'Golden Mean', which held that the aesthetic pleasure derived from a work was in direct proportion to the ratio of elements within it. Yet the ratio in question here directly concerns the relationship between man and nature, and the extent to which human destructiveness has overwhelmed nature, ironically impeding human attempts to gain wisdom through reading its patterns. A similar dynamic is traced in 'While Satyrs Hunted for a Nymph', where the philosophers' search for meaning finds a mirror in the beauty and particularity of the natural world. Such recognition is temporary however; Wingfield suggests that this search can never be over for the questing human subject.

III

More than ten years later Wingfield was still engaged by these questions, but by this stage her work had acquired a dark and anxious tone. During this time Wingfield's health had deteriorated considerably, with undiagnosed illnesses keeping her in seclusion for long periods. Whether as cause or effect of this malaise, her creative output declined considerably: *A Kite's Dinner: Poems 1938-54* was the Poetry Book Society's Choice in 1954, but it was essentially a selection from previous volumes, with just eight new poems included. The volume was poorly received by critics, and reinforced the impression of a poet whose career had slowed almost to a standstill. Elizabeth Jennings's judgement that Wingfield 'too rarely comes to grips with her subject matter' may misread the equivocation that was by then the hallmark of Wingfield's poetic voice, but it may also reflect the evident lack of creative momentum that she experienced at this time. In 1964 Wingfield, in correspondence with American John Lincoln Sweeney – curator of the Poetry Room at Harvard University – suggested that if he would read her poetry to date, and 'strike out' her bad work, she would have 'a very small collection to be remembered by'. Though somewhat melodramatic, this appeal hints at Wingfield's recognition that her creative life was largely in the past. The same year she changed publishers: *The Leaves Darken*, which came out in 1964 with Weidenfeld and Nicholson, reflects this continuing dark mood and moves closer to self-revelation than any other work she produced. 'Darkness' reprises earlier existential questioning but with a hopelessness now born of bitter experience. Doubting the capacity of faith or learning to provide lasting meaning, Wingfield begins to see emotional shortcomings as implicated in the fruitlessness of the search and directly addresses the ruinous character of destructive human behaviour:

With so much still unlearned, ignored;
So many moments of compassion skimped
By me or lost; this private graveyard seems
An apt memorial, with its church a ruin,
And its quiet cracked
By the quick clatter of black wings
In crude assault.

While the shape of the stanza enacts the retreat to privacy that Wingfield now found inevitable, she could no longer turn to Powerscourt House as the bulwark against exposure. Economic pressures, together with the irretrievable breakdown of her marriage led Wingfield to withdraw her financial support for the estate, causing it to be sold in 1961. Powerscourt was a place that, since her marriage, had crystallised Wingfield's hopes and fears for the future; her investment in it was emotional as well as monetary, and it expressed both her strong attachment to Ireland and her uneasy relationship with that country's past and present. The landscapes her poetry now depicts are desolate, and only with intense concentration can the grandeur of the past be recalled. 'For My Dead Friends' uncovers a Parthenon 'purged and marred' yet one that still causes 'a pain/Of exultation [to] grip/The midriff-soul with love'. Here Wingfield reprises lines she wrote some thirty years earlier in the poem 'Vivat'. She seemed to consider the published poem not as a fixed entity, but rather as a series of impressions or revelations that could be harnessed to new themes and forms.

As her own life became increasingly subject to unpredictable patterns, the subject of continuity began to preoccupy Wingfield creatively: the poem 'Continuity' meditates on the difficult relationship between the generations, the aged fearing the strength of the young. Anxiety is never far from Wingfield's work during this period, as the title poem of *The Leaves Darken* confirms: 'So, juices of the year/Dry into blacker leaf/And darker fear'. Her preoccupation with death has become more visceral, which in turn shows that her grasp of sensory immediacy had not diminished with age. 'Village Seasons' takes up this focus on the cycles of life – before 'huge fisted' death comes the beauty and particularity of each of the seasons in turn: spring hawthorns, summer mowing, autumn leaf fall and winter's hardened ground. Yet this awareness of cyclical progression now brings Wingfield back to the darkness of oblivion. 'The Fetch-light' concludes 'I crave one small/Owl-coin of Athens/To hold against/Calamities or just the dark'; next, 'Blinded Bird Singing' ends 'true night/Is never still,/Never such total dark'. The form of the poems themselves simplifies and contracts – shorter lines, a refined vocabulary, the single stanza – all testify to reduced expectation and endurance.

Yet, at the close of her writing life, Wingfield used this distillation of rich and troubled experiences to refine her interrogation of central human questions. Though by this time she was almost a forgotten figure in literary circles, she habitually turned to writing as a means to think more fully. In 'Waking', from *Admissions* (1977), she speaks of the need 'with all force possible' to '[t]ry out my tongue again'. The wish to turn always to poetry, no matter how challenging the circumstances, confirms the seriousness of Wingfield's art and her enduring attachment to poetic form and language as the means to investigate existential questions.

Yet in spite of the fact that the poet's concern with self had hardly lessened with time, this work shows her capable of close attention to the observable world, now usually directed towards life remembered, even though – as the poet herself declares in 'No Rusty Cry' – 'scavenging the past is wrong'. Though almost all these late poems were written in Switzerland, which would be Wingfield's home for most of the last twenty years of her life, many returned imaginatively to an Irish landscape. As 'Any Weekday in a Small Irish Town' demonstrates, Wingfield's preference for precise observation that deflects attention away from the speaking subject remained strong. Her ability to recognise the suffering of others had by now sharpened and her depiction of the donkey in this poem, '[w]earing blinkers cracked, old,/Askew, blocking one eye' and a bridle 'tight enough to smother:/You can see where it rubs' testifies to that sensitivity

– one that brings an added emotional dimension to these late works. Her concern with the destruction of creatures and landscapes became more pronounced and more urgent too: 'As the wild aurochs died;/And our elms. We have/Barely a minute now'. Yet in spite of these growing convictions, even at the very end of her career Wingfield saw self-knowledge as tentatively achieved – 'We die the moment that we start to learn/Just what we are, just where to turn'. That surprising 'what' reveals the scale of the poet's questioning: this is not the 'who' of personal reflection, but a larger enquiry into the human condition itself, and a vision of this condition as connected to the wider, more-than-human world. In spite of the seclusion of Wingfield's later life, her poetic impulse here is to continue the search for pattern and connection, a search which enriched the form and language of her poetry, and one which she would pursue to the end of her days.

Further Reading and Media

Boland, Eavan, 'A Latin Poet: A Lost Encounter', in *A Journey with Two Maps: Becoming a Woman Poet* (Manchester: Carcanet Press, 2011), 232-245.

Collins, Lucy, *Poetry by Women in Ireland: A Critical Anthology 1870-1970* (Liverpool: Liverpool University Press, 2012).

Davis, Alex, 'Wilds to Alter, Forms to Build: The Writings of Sheila Wingfield', *Irish University Review* 31.2 (Autumn/Winter 2001): 334-352.

'Hiding in Plain Sight: Sheila Wingfield.' *RTÉ Arts Lives*. Dir. Anne Roper. Radio Telefís Éireann, Dublin. Feb. 20, 2007. Television.

Perrick, Penny, *Something to Hide: The Life of Sheila Wingfield, Viscountess Powerscourt* (Dublin: Lilliput Press, 2007).

Wingfield, Sheila, *Admissions* (Dublin: Dolmen Press, 1977).
—, *Beat Drum, Beat Heart* (London: Cresset Press, 1946).
—, *A Cloud Across the Sun* (London: Cresset Press, 1949).
—, *Collected Poems 1938-1983*, preface by G. S. Fraser (New York: Hill and Wang, 1983).
—, *Her Storms* (Dublin: Dolmen Press, 1977).
—, *A Kite's Dinner: Poems 1938-54* (London: Cresset Press, 1954).
—, *The Leaves Darken* (London: Weidenfeld and Nicholson, 1964).
—, *Poems* (London: Cresset Press, 1938).

From *Poems*
(1938)

Odysseus Dying

I think Odysseus, as he dies, forgets
Which was Calypso, which Penelope,
Only remembering the wind that sets
Off Mimas, and how endlessly
His eyes were stung with brine;
Argos a puppy, leaping happily;
And his old Father digging round a vine.

Winter

The tree still bends over the lake,
And I try to recall our love,
Our love which had a thousand leaves.

The Change

As after journeys, candlelit, through books,
We long for morning ploughland and the rooks;
As summer that delays in listless air
Makes welcome ragged autumn, and the spare,
Blue smoke of woods; as we can know delight
In many musks and clamours of a night
Whose crowds are padding by a gleaming dome,
And yet soon miss the empty street of home,
With its far tap of footsteps on the kerb
That can no sleeping house or soul disturb;
As after steaming plains, the mountain's chill
Renews us: so do we, who have been ill
With love, awake at last unfevered, sane
As limpid air that has been washed by rain.

Chosroe the Second

In bedstuffs of brocade he lies
Unmoving, while his shadowed eyes
Can only stare
Through darkness. For a screaming jay
That flashed from his son's head
To take the throne as prey,
Keep him in his palace, and there
Starve him dead.

'The people smiled upon my son:
I feared and held his flutter in a cage.
They rose, imprisoned me; his rage
Making me carrion.
Oh, for the wind,
The bronze bit and the spume,
And earthy pebbles flying from our way;
Or could I lean
One moment from the windowsill
To snuff looseness of air that lies between
Orion and the medlar's bloom;
And cease to mind
That, carved in the bed's ornament,
These little squirrels still will play
Among their grapes when I am spent.'

So Chosroe grieves; until
For Caryatides he begs
With lifted arms and fluted legs,
To bear his sorrow through the night
On marble napes with all their might.
But from the pillared groves have flown

The twittering counsellors, and all
Is quiet as a forest, where alone
Slow-dropping fruits of hour or minute fall.

'It was a princely morning of bright winds
When flags, the horses of the air, were prancing mad,
That I inherited
The kingdom, glad
To send my armies striding like the sun,
Their cheeks now warmed by summer's grass
Of unknown kinds,
Now chilled by mountain pass,
Till Antioch and Damascus were outrun;
And leaving quays behind them bleached
Like bones, and streets dry as a riverbed, had reached
Chalcedon and beyond,
Three times. Then on to lands
For bases, among wind and sands
And creaking Phoenix palms, where the cicadas sing
Noisy as surf. My guards
Have watched the Hellespont, whose boats
When sailing westward
Touch salt-bitten leaves and seaweed floats
Up-river on the swell;
My embassies have been
Where little horsemen, for a moment seen,
Are swirled in mountain mist;
While here, as on a list
Of tumbled cities, I can spell
Jerusalem, whose shuffling crowds
I massacred to stain her floors
And take her Cross of the acacia tree;
Palmyra, empty but for a garrison
Who whistle in the open doors;

And unremembered spurs that winged me on
To the far hills or clouds.'

'"Sire, I find the skies in doubt
And statues weeping."
Suddenly our lances in the field
Rattled like leaves October winds have dried;
Now hawks and partridges that wheeled
Above the dancing blades could see
Our columns—usually a stream
That in its flow one moment parts
For hostile, elbowing rocks—
Were trickles, creeping,
Nearly drained, without a gleam;
Now, loudly as the shingle knocks
Beneath a drawn-up wave, our clashing pride
Was overwhelmed; and when, at Nineveh,
My troops that had set out
All scaled in armour like a morning sea,
By dusk lay on the plain with smoking hearts,
I knew my kingdom fallen like a tree.

'Back into the earth's caul
I shall soon go,
Leaving this useless air
To some old villager
Who sits against his cottage wall
And plantlike feels the wind and sun.
You gods of light and darkness, blow,
Blow on my little spark, so nearly done.'

Then Chosroe puts his cooling lips
Upon the black flute of the night, to dream
That his own breath

Becomes a tune that, coiling, drifts,
Unable to recall its theme,
Until in gentle rifts
Each moment thinner blown, it slips
Into the endless spaces of his death.

Young Argonauts

In a small bitterness of wind
The reeds divided, as we felt
Our keel slide over stones, and smelt

The lough all round us. Soon the trace
Of shore was further than the sight
Of wildbirds crying in their flight;

But now the waves are paler finned,
The water blacker, we are blown
To somewhere strange and yet foreknown:

This is the Euxine, this the place—
Row on, row on, to catch the gold
In dripping fleece, as they of old.

Highlander

And when he took his grief
Into the gentle-breasted hills,
He felt clouds marching, and the wind
Unheeded and unheeding pass
Through smallest bilberries in leaf
And the tough mountain grass,
Until he could no longer bear
The pressing of his soul,
And prayed to be released from self, from name,
To mingle senseless with the air
Some little time. But as within his mind
The oar would not desert its thole,
To his dark courtyard back he came
Uncomforted of all his ills.

The Dead

The wind that blew the plumes astray
And bore the trumpet noise away
Has so effaced the dead
And thinned them to so fine a mist
That, harried in a drove,
They run ahead.
This wind, from barrack square
Or from the asphalt near some tenement,
Does it persist
In hinting that each mortal should prepare
To shiver in a leafless grove?—
A jealous wind, that will steal half
Of the hot meadow's reaper-clack
Which is all summer, or the night-stock's scent,
Or, on the road, a friend's laugh,
And pleases to hurl back
Smoke or broken tiles where urchins shout;
Which turns a sleeper's thoughts to untrue shapes:
A stubborn wind, that thickens till you feel
A door bang. And then memory's shut out.

2

The quiet dead,
Who were decoyed by a false tale
Of murmurings on Lethe's pebbly bed,
Have cast from them as childishness our joy
In live and woken things which yet, may now
Be part of their own foolish, constant dreams;
And are aloof from how

We long to peer behind the murk
And pantomime of bony jowl
And yew and headstone, to unveil
Their voices or their children's screams,
Or how they hummed and paused at work.
But tautly as you dare to strain
In listening, you only hear again
Hector to Aias calling like an owl,
At night, across the windy plain of Troy.

3

In spite of it, so many of us strive
With vigour, when alive,
For marks of perpetuity;
In spite of knuckle-bones that lie
In hills, grass shuttered from the light;
In spite of that Imperial road
Where warriors stand in their huge stone
And wildflowers blow about their feet; in spite
Of nothing being colder than the rain
On knees of monuments, or mute as fame
From trumpets with the angel gilt;
Though manifold can be a name
As is the wind's print on the seas
And yet will fade in libraries,
Or few as those in thymy air
Found carved on a Pentelic chair;
Though this one is as neat
As a lark's shadow, that one grown
To a forbidding, dark domain;
Yet do we want some tower built,
Be it of moving, marching dust
Where soldiers tried, and failed, to make their thrust.

Sonnet (I)

Jordan that feeds from far Mount Hermon's snow,
Thames with its fogs and warehouses and docks,
Dargle whose alders dip on little rocks,
The Nile where heavily feluccas go,
Untroubled Avon in flat watermeadow
Or the mad pacing Rhine of many shocks,
Medway that swings the tackle through the blocks,
Deben now still, but for two boys who row;
The waters that will storm a city's gate
Or lie in glazing pools above a slope,
Or lessen, or become immoderate:
All these I feel within me and their scope
Carried by veins throughout my whole estate,
So quiet is my face and wild my hope.

The London Square

Come, Autumn, blow the sounds about
Of footsteps and of leaves,
For it is time we did without
The languor that deceives
Events with wishes, facts with doubt,
In the long summer eves;
Come, bring your blustering to rout
What softens or aggrieves.

Let a lad's whistle, scream of train,
Be carried on a gust
Of thought which snatches up the skein
Of what is hard and just;
Let pavements hiss in the night rain,
And tugboats hoot and thrust
Into our sleep, till we regain
Those dreams, for dream we must.

From *Beat Drum, Beat Heart*
(1946)

From Men in War

Brothers, this is our cloud, our hidden night.
We, being obscured ourselves, know nothing,
  In this darkness find no frame,
  No ladder to climb in clear air,
No tap or chip of bricks on a bright day;
But lean together as if chained to pillars,
  Under scourge from the whole world.
  And now not I, but at all cost
The other, must be saved from harm. Look how
In chaos they are carrying a boy
  On strong arms, with safe steps, or lifting
  In the half-drowned enemy,
Their names lost like a voice in the storm, shown
On the scroll of the sea, hushed in passages
  And space of air, of empty windy
  Air, or shouted in a noise
Uncurling to implacable explosion
And then vanished, gone. Note, in this turmoil,
  How it's strange as myth to meet
  A man who sows his land in calm,
A pigeon nest, joy of a watermill:
For in our blood we feel the heavy pace
  Of cataracts and, in our limbs,
  The tremor of small leaves that shake
Beside them, on their banks, perpetually.
We are a madness, shrill over the ground,
  We are the bass notes' melancholy;
  We are the men who pulled Lorca
Between shrubs, beyond night-shadowed houses;
We are a man dragged and killed on the outskirts
  Of a town in Spain. We also know

Much of the horror and the numbness—
Snow to the waist—of the defense of Moscow;
A shelterwarden's knack of seeming mild,
    His inner rage. Another time,
    Close under the soil we go
In trenches, huddled in a reek of furs,
Like pictures in a bestiary: for cunning,
    Fellowship and cruelty
    Live in my palms and shins and back;
And glitter-eyed, like flocks at night, are those
Who camp in dips and hollows of a field.
    Each thing that stirs, warily
    Is watched and feared and felt and spied,
And silence, or the din of gunfire, guessed
For signs. Sappers have kneeled; they tap and wait
    And listen for the faintest sounds,
    Then know their fate. O smile O cry
For minutes hang on rumours of a rumour,
Hours fall to a wreck, and seconds beat
    As in Cassandra's pulsing neck
    With my defeat or with your doom,
With answer to our two encountered ranks,
With hurts, much longing, sickness and huge dread.

From Men at Peace

So will a voice, at random
In the fields become
A structure of compassionate sounds
Which you will climb like ladders in the air,
Until the mighty, fugal arguments declare
You noble, sad and great.

So, in a Gothic window,
Virtue with all force must press
In power. Unquenched, the embers glow
Round Peter's robe that's greener than sea deeps;
Saint Eustace aims his shaft as the stag leaps
Through the Cathedral darkness and the dread.

So, if a Londoner,
You go from Amen Corner
Into Paul's, on up under the dome's
Vast hum of silence where the many tongues are tomes:
You sit among first books, and read, if you deserve,
Of *Troilus and Criseyde*, how the pen stabs with goodness
And undoes the nerve.

So, someone will detect
And map proportions that connect
New threads of reasoning and light
Moving unceasingly in growth, or in the sea's
Suspense, in stars that comb the air with tracks
And problems as with parallax.

So the lens grinder, blest in name, in soul,
In understanding of our load

Of human plight,
And for defining attribute and mode
Of God into one luminous, transparent whole,
Stays gentle and upright.

From Women in Love

I said inspired: fully
   I mean it. Each word,
Each event, shows me its own,
   Natural tact;
From chance, or proper command,
   I am the elect.
My devotion is felt as it watches
   The pale young preacher
Who climbed to the pulpit,
   A rose in his mouth—
And look how confidence
   Can lie in my hand
That's loose and open, power
   Along my arm
Smoother than lip of a shell;
   And how my gladness
Breaks the sea in spurts
   Of dolphin foam.
How easy to move, to act!
   Forebodings have fled
As bat-form shreds of cloud
   Escape at sunrise;
What was difficult
   Is plain as noonday
Heat in light that dazzles
   The lost marshes,
Over which our thoughts
   Shake in the air
Like larks: this light, strong
   As was the vision
That Aquinas saw

Who then fell silent
To dispute no more.
    This light gives glory,
Lustre, unity—
    Wakens the Future
From half-lidded sleep:
    Who, with his eyes
Near blinded by behests
    And glare, shuts them,
Deciding to impose
    The shadow of old
Debts, policies,
    And doubts again.

From Women at Peace

She has reached
The rim of time
The dune end
Of the world.
Spiked grass
Loose sand
What to lean on
Where to turn ...
Something recalled
Before it is known,
Old as the ground,
New as herself
But sharp and steep
As memories
Of crag and shelf
In witless sheep
Who make their mountain
Tracks on a low
Mound, of rushing
Wind in ducks
Who are now placid
On the pond
But once were wilder
Than the air—
Some voice in her
That tries to find
And utter the old
Chants, the old
Pain, cries out:

O random Fate, who rout
And shatter and unbind
The elbow-leaning, tame,
Demurest pieties—
Free me that I may wear
A yoke I hanker for
And name: precise belief
In the authority
And overbearing deeds
Of a loved mortal, one
Whose strength and tongue shall be
The provenance of right;
A part in all transactions
Of his mind and any
Tragedies which follow.
Admit that the devout
Must have sanction from Church,
A thief from others' failings,
The privileged from custom,
Scholar from book—and I
From discipline of great
And terrible truths. Hold me,
Pour back my soul, let me know
Life the unfinished: so
Reflood the desolate ebb:
Renew me, make me whole.

From *A Cloud Across the Sun*
(1949)

Ireland

This is the country
That has no desolation, no empty feel
(The pagan kings are always there)
In ruined abbey, ruined farmhouse,
Slab of cromlech, or a wheel
Travelling a bog road
Through Calary's too quiet air.

Any Troubled Age

O mussel-coloured houses by the dunes
With fluttered boats feeling among the shoals,

How many times can it have happened,
How many times

O mountain straked and softened by blue air
With trickles fingering between the reeds,

How many times can it have happened,
How many times

O cottage field warmed by the breath of sheep
When rain begins to gossip in the hedge,

How many times will woman see
Some man trudging

To the door, and rise, with a broken welcome—
For the whole news has travelled in his eyes.

Architectural Tour

A pillar wrecked
By sand; the slat
Of softest leaves
To hide a voice
And hint its echo;
Pediments
Where hogmaned ponies
Prance in fat
Of stubbornness;
Or the stones
Of Clonmacnois,
Lichen-flecked;
Cupolas that
Burst through snow;
Spires where angels
Catch their gowns;
Tin-roofed chapels
In sick towns—
A choice,
A guess.

Ross Abbey

The cowpat track and dusty bramble leads
To childhood's riverwet and glistening meads.
O dear Ross Abbey! ruined, with a tree
Grown through you, how your presence lived in me
With images, persistent and devout,
Of a loved brother, weed and frog and trout,
Until that middle-aged, that rainy day
I saw you once again, then looked away.

Sectio Divina

The heart sings
Of Colchis in whose forests once wild aurochs hid
    Till Jason ploughed with them—
    O happy farmer Jason;
    And the splashed hem
    Of barefoot women on
A shore, stooping, looking for octopus or squid
  While the sea rages to condemn
    All tamed and gentle things.

Because of savagery preferred,
Gone the lost cause, the trusting bird:
Gone the cahòws and their strange cry,
Gone from Bermuda; in our eye
Life's image lies reversed, while slaughter
Rules the air, the ground and water.

    Cures are found
In plants, or else where beaches lie most derelict.
    Gaze, soul, at the spiral
    Of a shell; count
    In the fircone's numeral
    How gnomons can surmount
Opposing forces with the mediating, strict
  And Golden Mean, whose wiles are all
    Displayed in tide and ground.

Origins

1

Thinness of music far away—
Repeated thuds, a few high notes,
Are all one hears—how well this teases
Memory, angers the brain.
Towards me in the same way floats
A sense of forbears long ago
Distressing as that distant playing:
For it can never be made clear,
What did our predecessors fear?
How did they sleep? When did they smile?
Were they uneasy in their souls?

2

A wind blows along the quays.
Rigging slats. Hawsers creak.
Here they stumble: in big hands
Smaller hands that pinch and tweak;
Coming from the barest mountain
Or a quiet of flat lands
To cities smoking in the dusk,
To pestilence and grime that's both
On water and the merchant-desk:
These ancestors, these falling leaves
That as they rot make green my growth.

3

Before them—pedlar, diplomat,
Landlord, peasant—these talk low,
Whistle, curse, stamp their feet;

That one greasy as his hat,
This one laughing from conceit.
All mine. As for the women: some
Have a scent of melancholy sedge,
Or laurels in wet woods; others
Rock slowly on high balconies
Under a charring sun; and some
Are rags along a gutter's edge.

4

Could quick, varied contradiction
Of a mood or thought derive from difference
Of fancies they were racked with—could
It stem from their belief in arches
Made of angels' wings, from fret
Of learning, or from schemes sad
As rain falling from winter larches?
And some ghastly call of wit
Come from where there was a joke
Before a murder—now where flit
Jackdaws in the ivied tower?

5

Beyond such silting up, such tracts
Of time and back to paradisal
Leaves: this moist and sheltering sight
Of the great garden, dense, entire
With fruit all year, and flying lizards
Settling in the tree of life,
Wings folded; and the sweet thorn-apple
Sharpening minds into a knife—
This land which none need go from, past
The distant, guardian sword of fire
That wavers to the left and right.

6

However vast and ancient are these
Epochs, all of them seem mirrored
In my temper, which can feel
Walled in, or else defenceless, eager
And thrusting like armies, soft as sand,
Cast down like cities; never still
But moving on to a new land
Or climate, all in a few hours—
Contracted yet exact, as after
Rain the storm-filled sky lours
In the smallest rut. But if

7

There were an age yet earlier,
North of the dank Caucasian pass,
Before the everburning fields
And Tartarus the triple-moated
Town, and near the iron-throated
Mountain coughing brass and steel—
Then, as a woman, I have found
What we inherit in our blood,
From those bereaved by the first waste
And wailing for their menfolk drowned
In utter darkness of the flood.

While Satyrs Hunted for a Nymph

While satyrs hunted for a nymph
(We, for wild strawberries in a wood)
Philosophers, their blood and lymph
Excited by the search for Good,

Found Cause in Space; and tracked Despair
In Time; felt human Destiny
And Reason swaying in the air
Like a bee-tumbled peony;

Perceived (but never told their School)
Truth transparent as a shrimp
Darting backwards in a pool;
And Thought with all its tendons limp.

They are gone. Their counter-pleas
Of proof have left us, every one,
Like sailors whistling for a breeze—
And still the breeze drops with the sun.

Even So

In spite of striding
Lean-legged John's
Flaming words
In the wilderness;

And orators
Who stand in bronze,
Braving both
The rain and birds—

None the less,
Just as dogs
Prefer to lap
In filthy puddles,

So the fishwives'
Hands will chap,
Roofs fall loose
And walls get sick.

In spite of garlic
Breath of Rome
And senators;
In spite of lives

Good as a fable;
Envoys, tired
And fidgeting
At a treaty table—

Children still
Have pecked-out lungs;
The old maid slanders
All around;

Hope like a fox,
Has gone to ground;
And crowds feel hate
That burns their tongues.

Poisoned in Search of the Medicine of Immortality

When Hsüang Tsung, great emperor,
Giddy and ill, carried in a litter,
Saw the stars sway,

His conquests and his arguments
And powers, falling into fever with him,
Pulsed their lives away.

Bow to his shade. To be at rest
Is but a dog that sighs and settles: better
The unrelenting day.

Epiphany in a Country Church

Rough-fisted winter and the blurred organ join
In minds of villagers to bring
A smell of wheatstraw under hoofs and sanfoin
In hay where beasts are fattening.

What does it matter if our wise men stress
The Barn as false, the Feast as wrong?
I hold the Magi were the wiser, yes,
To be believed in for so long.

A January mist now hides the wood;
Hard facts are overlaid by myth:
In us these last keep company, and should,
Like heart and bones in Farmer Smith

Who kneels to pray. Rubbing his neck—If beef
Goes up this month, he thinks . . . Round him
Confer vague consolations, powers of grief,
Man's fear and the high cherubim.

War and Peace

'Lately I cried with men.
Now once again
I wait for the slack of the tide,
Watch for a smooth in the wave and drop
My lobsterpots
Down between the grey rocks:
In the wet rope
Strong hope.'

'The violence I was in,
Its crash and din
Are gone. My dear one, nothing breaks
When she holds it, or tumbles from her lap
Save when she starts up
Quickly to greet me or give me to sup:
In the folds of her dress
Gentleness.'

The Dog

1

Calm in their age, these city walls
Stand with full dignity at night,
Consoling men for what appals
And horrifies the waking sight.

2

Far down, low in the ditch, by stones
This urban power is founded on,
Some dog, sniffing for scraps or bones,
Feeling a sudden apprehension,

3

Yelps. And gathers answering yelp
And bark to reassure it. Oh
My soul, what can I do to help
Your guilt that lurks and runs below?

Funerals

Be done with show. Let the dead go to their lair
Unseen, a step barely heard on the stair.

From *A Kite's Dinner*
(1954)

Ease

By skilled pretence of conjuring one hour
    Of wholly unmolested power,
I call for noon prolonged. And let it be
    The summer of my days; agree
To flowering lindens where bees overflow;
    Or shade of currants, where I go;
Let seeding grasses touch my legs and nudge
    Their plumes: that Rhadamanthus, judge
And ruler in Elysian fields, may bless
    Such clear and easy happiness.

Rid of ambition—and the hope that fame
    Might one day mouth my whispered name—
I find delusion and her sighs in flight;
    Then gently as the sea at night
Breathes on a southern shore, the senses fall
    Assenting and forgiven. All
Who travelled home on hay-floats, warm and tired
    Will know my thoughts: this calm desired,
That gains sufficient strength to climb the steep
    Smooth orchard ladder into sleep.

A Tuscan Farmer

Why praise the huge past works of Hercules
When he leans idly on his club in Rome?
Come to my farm instead; walk round my home
When autumn puts its ladder in the trees
And what was stripped two thousand years ago
Is stripped again, or ploughed, made into stacks
And ricks and bundled heaps, by arms and backs
Aching with thrift. The least of plants that grow
As fodder have to fight the drought: my oxen,
Walking softly, pull with as great a strain.
Each clod, and hanging leaf, and wild grass cane
Is stronger than that strongest of all men
Whose lion, hydra, hell-dog, mares and boar
Were overcome indeed, but once, no more.

Janus

A draught blown
Through January's door
Touches hard eyelids, chilled by night,
Of Two-Face, overseer
And guardian, who has always known
That warm and secret rite
Behind him, and the clear
Sharp light
Of any coming year.
Along this street, poor
Shutters, all thrown
Crookedly together, have their hinges closed
On shames, joys,
Longing, dread,
Restless and exposed
In dreams whose poise
Tilts back then leans ahead—
As if souls could explore
And fly in shuttlecock and battledore
Between life and the dead.
Till the town grumbles, clatters, gains its sight
And the last sleeper shakes,
Opens his mouth, wakes
And, jumping out of bed,
Uncombs the tangled morning noise.

2

And what if ships
Should break the distant skin of the sea?

Or plague or worm provide
Disaster for each olive-tree?
That is a last year's story
As today our lips
Forget rope, wind and tide,
Reasons and orders, while they speak
Of what we see:
A drop of water
Trembling in its slide
Along a sparrow's beak;
The blowsy girl who'll tweak
And laugh, pulling a little daughter
By her dress
Back to the old one's hips
Sunk down in massive happiness;
Or of a child who runs
With gutter treasure
To his mother while her face is like the sun's
Full pleasure
As her arms and knees
Jiggle the baby: fondness
Has no measure:
Newness no comparisons.

Calendar

1

Too clean, the infant year, too new
And snowy innocent: it hides from view
Old rooted grudge and sin.

2

But memory floods to an edge
Of dark and bitter February sedge
That shivers like our skin,

3

And doubts are colder than the hands
Of men who harrow the long pasturelands
In painful discipline:

4

Until high mercy will assuage
The heart, and show it April's missal-page
Alive upon the ground.

5

Lovers now welcome thunderskies:
Their shock, the shelter, and a flash of eyes
That can be strange, profound,

6

Then tender as the fledgling days
Of June, when beauty trembles in the haze
With every rustling sound.

7

The halfway month. A pause for fears
Of middle-age, a deskful of arrears,
Time sped, so little done,

8

As heat lies heavy on the land.
Dogs snap at flies. Few tempers can withstand
The slowness of the sun,

9

Or parks that shrivel, leaves that spoil,
The sad allotments dug in a sour soil
Where towns and grime have won:

10

We need to feel gross sacks of grain
And in them, deities of earth and rain,
To put our sickness right.

11

The cake is crumbling, fires are lit.
Pink-pawed and back humped up, a mouse will sit
And nibble in quick fright;

12

And old, fat-fingered oaks are bare
While stars wheel through the empty, frozen air
To the slow hum of night.

From *The Leaves Darken*
(1964)

Darkness

And what will mitigate my life's long fault,
    I beg you, if authority's black stuffs
    Should fail to reconcile me
    To the final blindfold?
    Cassock and mortar-board
    Are under the same burden,
    Suffer the same problem, as ourselves;
    While conscience comes at night and stings
    The darkness: much as Carthage, ploughed under,
    Was then sown with salt.
A conjuror's cloak; the Queen of Spades
    With her poor migraine face: these
    Are for innocence: it waits agog,
    For flourishes of fireworks to exalt
    A pitchblack sky. Later,
    Incredible beliefs, the greatest things
    Given to the soul, are only
    Metaphors or hints
    Taken from lovers when they meet
    Bemused, in gardens,
    Among mooncast shadows
    Denser than a vault.
Let me predict my funeral weather
    Biting at black coats,
    With the new box—cave dark and cupboard thick—
    Brought to a lurching halt
    Near brambles and tipped headstones in the family
    Burial ground, and flurryings
    Of shocked and interrupted jackdaws...
With so much still unlearned, ignored;
    So many moments of compassion skimped

By me or lost; this private graveyard seems
An apt memorial, with its church a ruin,
And its quiet cracked
By the quick clatter of black wings
In crude assault.

Cartography

1

To map out man or woman,
Let your nervous hand try to lead
Wisdom by a twisted forelock.
Find what injuries were done
To self-esteem: redress
The boundary; give fads attention.
Measure out loneliness.
If you hold the plan
Still workable, think how a weathercock
Will rule an empty street at night;
Or that a smudge of print can cite
Those full extravagancies
Waiting in a grub; or plant-seed;
Or the mind—
Wild as equinoctial seas—
Of ordinary humankind.

2

A boat slewed
Towards the urgent flood,
Its anchor fluke dragging mud
And cable fouled: that goes for most of us. We risk
Mishandling time, whose hurry
Carries off branch, bole, root, in spate.
I've watched rank pulled away, near tamarisk
And the Bermudian tides, where a proconsul made
Gestures too old and negligent;
And there, known a massive brain prematurely
Crumble in wrecker's dust;

Learnt how young sailors dropped, beside a carronade
And hulk, on sand: no moment
Being right or just.
While coral of praise or gratitude
(You've guessed) can come too late.

3

Does this smack
Overmuch of water? But one's
Life can be a voyage
To Cythera: in black
Storms; faint calm; or else uneasy from cross-currents
Of what's difficult or fluent.
As there's no finish to our quirks, beliefs,
Distorted theories and failing reasons,
We might embark
For coasts that wear a greener plume,
Where caverns rest the mind in dark,
Leaving a crystal-shattered spume
Outside. No light can gauge
Hollows and sudden gaps, or chart
Those devious reefs
And unsure soundings of one person's heart.

For My Dead Friends

Fit for a knacker's yard,
This carcase of a poor
Parthenon, purged and marred,
Is such a prodigy
None can feel condescending. From its floor,
Where wagtails run and dip
In marble puddles after morning rain,
Columns empower the air with flesh,
Not stone, tender and fresh:
Making a pain
Of exultation grip
The midriff-soul with love.
Where to turn, giddy from shock?
Below, a woman spins, shouts to a neighbour;
Children play. High, high above,
Sea-eagles, circling slowly, eye with disfavour
Any shell left chipped and empty
On a rock.

So, harassed puny man
Has built, ennobling the weak moment.
Taking stock, we can
Jot down that in no matter what ironic
Landscape people work and die—
The serious, foolish, modest, lewd,
The bold or shy, violent or subdued,
With their diversity of features,
Humours, failures—

They have renewed
Their pity and are found
Forgiving God each tragic,
Tearing thing,
Throat swollen and voice faltering
From gratitude.
What more should I,
Muddled and earthbound,
Need for the soul's nourishment?

3

In spite of which I waste
My breath, and spill live sorrow on the thought
That we, who carry friends
Like a good taste
In the mouth, so short a time, ought
To be left, not random odds and ends
For a remembrance, not a shard
Stupidly small and hard,
But an emphatic plier
That can wrench the mind, turn it and amaze;
Some elegiac force
Whose lunge and potency
Could lather Phaethon's reins, each horse
Sun-bent though undisastrously:
More than Achilles felt when mountain flanks
Showed muletracks, scarred all sideways,
To get planks
To feed Patroclus' fire.

4

The pen scratches and flies drone
And towns suffer heat,

And I know life can be weariness
And the sour pleasure of the incomplete.
To ease it calls for metaphor.
I'll take, then, for my own
Hand, the Parthenon, that hollowness
Above new Athens, quite distinct
From the complexity
Spread out beneath, but linked
With every roof and hearth, as what is true
Should be; that shell
Now flushed by haze, colour of asphodel—
And pick it up, and hold it to my ear
Whenever, privately, I wish to hear
Its murmur celebrate
Those whom I knew
Who were both good and great.

Continuity

When morning came lightly as a hare's breath,
Worry held us
In its copper snare
With a sick pull of death.
We were alone
Under the anger of old people and their
Bias. Now, walking crookedly,
We're mottle-red;
Shrunk or paunchy;
Brittle as curled-up leaves; or rancorous;
Others ghastly,
Like a bone:
Fearing our sons and their bold, brilliant stare.

A Query

Rusted, small, weed-hidden
And unlocked, forgotten:
Such was the backdoor
Of the unbelievable Byzantine citadel.
So when Turks elbowed through it, grunting, to dispel
This blaze unseen before—
A jewel-hung emperor as Christ Pantokrator—
Who were the faithful, who the infidel?
Experts are cunning and say nothing more.

The Leaves Darken

If a child's tale were sung
To kings and the tired spearmen;
Or if Outer Isles, fog-blind,
Are found only by raven
Croaks; or a new housing scheme should geld
Some king-cup creek;
If Menelaus hung
His head in Egypt
After war was done,
While gnats, then flies, sipped
His blood by night and blistering sun
Until those bony temples held
Ideas that were quite brittle, hollow, weak;
As an old parrot tears a rind
From sugary belief—
So, juices of the year
Dry into blacker leaf
And darker fear.

Village Seasons

A gauzewing fly lights on my hand;
Birds echo; wildest promises abound
And hawthorn creams the land.

Summer, lazing on her elbow,
Watches unremitting mowers, thirsty,
Dazed, work to and fro.

Gold coins—a fortune—drop from trees
Into ditch-coffers underneath the ash
That dangles rusty keys.

Now pumps wear topknots made of straw
And roads clang underfoot; young cheeks shine red,
Bright as a hedge haw.

But cottage Death, huge fisted, wrings
The sheet out when it pleases her, intent,
Intent on other things.

Sonnet (II)

I'll speak of Alexander's honied corpse;
Or Arthur's well-gashed skull, with one dint raw
The day they buried him; what Phaedra saw
From behind leaves: for these are fibres, warps
And chains connecting every creature's soul
Inside humanity; never outdated,
But as horrible as streets of slated
House-rows in Victorian grime and role
Of industry, which had no Artemis:
Only an upright piano and the hymns.
I'll speak of these, then ask: When heads or limbs
Are lopped in private hate and war, is this
More terrible in hills, or where men mow,
Or Mons, or Troy, or mound of Jericho?

An Answer from Delphi

1

To keep a balance and to bear
The world; its disarray;
Its wounds; its many failures
Of attempts to supplicate untold
Divergencies of gods angry or gay,
Innocent or shrewd
By souls a hotch-potch of what's bold,
Eager, alarmed, submissive, wily, crude—
We know such warring humours
Have to be resolved. But where?

2

Beneath a gold mosaic, spanned
By plainchant, resonant with praise
And punishment? Or in
Aeolian islands, ridden by winds, by brightness,
The Bermudas, when a conch shell brays?
Where sages struck a chill
In Ireland's side, through hound, princess
And cattle-thieves, with a strong, holy quill?
Under the salt and skin
Of Jutish estuary land?

3

Parnassos and its rocks resound
With cries of little birds,
Diminished priests of Apollo.
Poverty must work to mule-bells and the clear
Water's tumble. No Castalian words

Are needed to contain
One riddle by another: here,
Sacred and common are conjoined and plain,
While feathery tremors grow
From olive trees clenched in the ground.

Common Wish

Love plays in the sun,
Sickens, droops and is done.
    A spider's thread
Rolls up, binds up her dead.
    There is too much
For us between a dockleaf's touch
And Saturn, which with frosty rings
In utter darkness whirls and stings.

Gleam candour, friend,
Blush to the very end,
    Alert and quick
And warm as a hind's lick
    Over her calf
To comfort it. Keep near. Then half,
A third, the whole of us could choose
To sop, not crack, our mortal bruise.

From *Her Storms*
(1977)

Clonmacnois

Along the gently
Sloping riverbanks
Of Shannon with its placid flow
And all its wildfowl,
Why should the ruins
Of Clonmacnois,
Pillaged by savages
When most renowned and holy—
Why do its ravages,
In fact,
Make the heart easy
With high calm, tact
And harmony?

Not Forgetting Aeneas Sylvius

Not forgetting Aeneas Sylvius—
Novella writer and then Pius the Second—
Gloriously borne aloft
Into the Lateran's basilica
To face a sacristan who knelt
Holding a wisp of burning cotton on a pea-stick:
Totter-man, or throne, needs a reminder
Of how short is triumph,
How it never condescends.

Tyranny

Antigone's no rebel:
She must fulfil
The ancient rite.
She cannot leave
Her brother to the kites.
In spite of Creon, walling-up
And death by hanging, she
Did manage—just—to put
Some small earth over him.
Before dogs found the body.

History lacks a Teiresias
To speak our future.

How then to fend off tyrants?
Proteus in sea-caves,
Old Proteus, will not say
Although he knows;
But glides into an undertow,
Flits over sand, or flows
Beneath the pride
And camber
Of a wave, hiding
From questioners.

Carpaccio

St. Ursula dreaming
And the little dog guarding her
Neither are disturbed
By that gentle
Angel of death who opens the door
Quietly

Then on a day
That has each pennant flapping
She embarks on the green sea of Venice
To be martyred in Cologne
Her host of companions
Killed with her

Eleven thousand virgins
Or so it goes
Totally absurd you think
But what a pinprick beside
Each fatuous intake
Of each common breath

Brigid

Brigid, once
Protector of poets;

Patron of Kildare
Where nowadays foxhounds

Keep muzzles down to the scent
While bullocks fatten;

Worshipped by Romans
Under Severus in York;

Protector from domestic fires
In Ireland
And now its own saint;

Lady, I bow to your diversity.

St. Francis

St. Francis when he lay blinded
Hated mice.
They ran off with his bread.
Never would he laud them
Or call them brother.

With his eyes cured
There were the birds of course
Also bed-bugs and fleas
And pebbles on the road
Lodging in his sandals
To preach to
And profess his love for.

But not one good word
Did he have
For the wise and patient
Overloaded donkeys
Red with sores
And bruised by sticks
That he met
On the long way to Rome
And back.

The Fetch-Light

Known as a fetch-light
And omen of death,
A gleam floating
Through the winter night
Over some rooftop,
Tillage, copse or park,
Was only a harmless owl gliding
With its feathers luminescent
From a rotted stump.

I crave one small
Owl-coin of Athens
To hold against
Calamities, or just the dark.

Blinded Bird Singing

This blinded bird singing,
What can he think about,
Pinioned by a cage? God's grief,
How can he sing? Without
Miltonic, high extravagance
Of learning, still
He exults, hailing
The holy light
As if each quill
Could feel its way between
A branch and leaf
Where tree-wasps dance
And grubs are found
Under the bark
By a keen
Prising bill,
And every thicket seen
Has its own multitudes of sound,
And night—true night
Is never still,
Never such total dark.

One's Due

Wife-beaters of course and constant liars,
The delicately mean or wilfully feeble,
People bent on provoking a child's scream
Or its future downfall,
Those sick with envy
And the high boasters,
Merit that burning rubbish-dump
Of stinking corpses, sewage and offal
In the long ditch running below Jerusalem,
Known as Ge-Hinnom.

I should be there
For a heap of quiet crimes:
Chances of good aborted
When my tongue was too quick
Or my heart too slow,
The lost moment,
Unmeant betrayals from sheer
Inadvertence or stupidity—
Huge or trifling,
These too call for the pit.

View

At the sea's edge, near Bray
In County Wicklow,
From a lonely
Field for dumping rubbish,
Water and air seemed shining, pearly,
Still. No sound.
Gulls rode the gentlest swell
Of this small estuary.

Nearby in Rocky Valley
Among small concrete homes
Fenced round with wire,
One could smell
Bracken and a few sheep, and see
Both copper domes of Powerscourt
Rising over the haze, far off.
Domes and domesticity, entire
As stallions, but now
Burnt to the ground.

A Melancholy Love

Part elegant and partly slum,
Skies cleaned by rain,
Plum-blue hills for a background:
Dublin, of course.
The only city that has lodged
Sadly in my bones.

In a Dublin Museum

No clue
About the use or name
Of these few
Bronze Age things,
Rare
And in gold,
Too wide for finger-rings.
Till some old epic came
To light, which told
Of a king's
Daughter: how she slid them on to hold
The tail ends of her plaited hair.

From *Admissions*
(1977)

Waking

When Lazarus
Was helped from his cold tomb
Into air cut by bird-calls,
While a branch swayed
And the ground felt unsteady:
I must, like him, with all force possible
Try out my tongue again.

Any Weekday in a Small Irish Town

A rusty, nagging morning.
By the pub's
Front door, now shut,
An ass-cart waits and waits.
This scrap of donkey
Wearing blinkers cracked, old,
Askew, blocking one eye,
Has also a string
Bridle pulled on crookedly
And tight enough to smother:
You can see where it rubs.

At dusk, cornerboys
So shy
And full of silent hates,
Get lanced by rain and cold.
They stand beside
The factory gates
Before the shift goes off,
Scowling at each other.
Girls hurry out
Together, giggling by.
And still the donkey waits.

Remote Matters

As long as I can kneel to tell
Pin-eyed from thrum-eyed primroses
Or find a small cranesbill
In rough grass,
Why should I mind
If Dunwich is under the sea
With nine churches drowned?

Sparrow

Slim, chic and pale,
This young sparrow looks, pecks, looks.
His beak and my thumbnail
Are made of the same stuff,
Spin with the same atoms.
How can I understand,
While my finger turns a bookleaf,
That for him seeds and quick sips
Of water are enough?

No Rusty Cry

No rusty cry
From corncrakes in a field of wheat—
Their thin legs could outrun
And would defy
The reaper's clack
That spoke for summer's
Lazy heat.
Combine harvesters
Have come along
And must be best.

Though scavenging the past is wrong—
I can't go back,
I have no rest—
Where is the future's drowsy sun?
What will be fresh, untainted, blest?

From *Cockatrice and Basilisk*
(1983)

Destination

The ladder has been left slanted
In a half-clipped hornbeam
And a rake's teeth
Will no more scratch gently across the gravel.

Rows of defective houses
Wait until they're crushed
In rubble-dust.
To slums, or unkempt gardens, all of us travel.

Urgent

Villages pass under the plough
In England, where there was plague,
And lets time slide over parishes
The way hedges are torn out.
Bulldozers flatten a hill:
Even continents slip.
Everything must elide or kill
As the wild aurochs died;
And our elms. We have
Barely a minute now.

No Instructions

To give quite freely or else hold,
To be amazed, or bold:

How can we judge? Connect
Our body's bias, dogma, sect?

Once, Dr Dee's high-polished coal
Played mirror. We have quasar or black hole

For marvel. Not a thing
Is understood. And, ripening,

We die the moment that we start to learn
Just what we are, just where to turn.

Notes

Odysseus Dying

Odysseus, hero of Homer's *Odyssey*, is most famous for his ten-year journey home following the Trojan Wars. In this poem it is not his sexual encounters that he remembers, but his early experiences of place and family.

Mimas: a district in Turkey.

Chosroe the Second

Chosroe (or Khosrau) *II* was King of Persia from 590 to 628. Though he presided over many military victories he was not himself a warrior, relying instead on the strategies of his generals. He was known for his arrogance and for his love of luxury. The end of Chosroe's reign is likened to the decay and death of winter, suggesting the cyclical nature of kingship.

Orion: a constellation at the edge of the Milky Way, interpreted as a hunter.

Medlar: a tree similar to the hawthorn, native to south-east Europe and western Asia.

Caryatides: female figures used as columns to support an entablature.

Antioch: an ancient city on the eastern side of the Orontes River, near the modern city of Antakya in Turkey.

Damascus: capital of Syria; one of the oldest continuously inhabited cities in the world.

Chalcedon: an ancient maritime town in Asia Minor, almost directly opposite Byzantium.

Hellespont: the ancient name of the narrow passage between the Aegean Sea and the Sea of Marmara.

Palmyra: earlier in Chosroe's reign this was an important city in central Syria.

Nineveh: the site of Chosroe's final defeat.

Young Argonauts

Euxine: another name for the Black Sea, which Jason sailed in search of the Golden Fleece.

Highlander

thole: a vertical pin or peg in the side of a boat against which the oar presses during the act of rowing.

The Dead

Part 1
plumes: an ornamental arrangement of feathers worn ceremonially. These were often attached to the heads of horses pulling a hearse.

reaper-clack: the sound of a mechanical reaper. The persona of the reaper is associated with death.

Part 2
Lethe: a river in Hades. Drinking its waters induced forgetfulness of the past.

Hector and *Aias* (or Ajax): fought two important contests during the Trojan War; these are represented in Virgil's *Iliad*.

Part 3

Pentelic: from Mount Pentelicus, near Athens. Often designates objects made from the famous white marble quarried there.

Sonnet (I)

The poem names eight rivers in all, from the biblical River Jordan to the Dargle that rises in the Wicklow Mountains and flows over Powerscourt waterfall, on the estate that Wingfield's husband inherited in 1947. As well as major rivers such as the Nile, the Rhine and the Thames, the poem names three less well-known English rivers.

Feluccas: small vessels propelled by oars and/or lateen sails.

From Men At Peace

Amen Corner: to the west of St *Paul's* Cathedral in London. On the feast of Corpus Christi monks would process from Paternoster Row to St Paul's: the 'amen' at the conclusion of the Our Father would occur as they turned this corner.

lens grinder: Baruch Spinoza (1632-1677), Jewish-Dutch philosopher.

Ireland

cromlech: prehistoric megalithic structure.

Calary: townland south of the Powerscourt estate.

Any Troubled Age

straked: marked with lines; streaked.

Architectural Tour

hogmaned: with a mane that stands erect.

Clonmacnois: 'A monastic university founded in the sixth century by St

Ciaran, a centre of scholarship and manuscript making, repeatedly raided by Danes, then Irishmen, and finally sacked by the English.' [original note]

Ross Abbey

Ross Abbey is among the best-preserved Franciscan friaries in Ireland. It is located near Cong in County Galway.

Sectio Divina

Originally titled 'The Heart Sings'.

Sectio Divina or 'Divine section' was another term for the Golden Ratio or Golden Mean. According to this mathematical rule, aesthetic pleasure is determined by the ratio of elements within the created work.

Colchis: the home of Medea and the destination of the Argonauts.

aurochs: the ancestors of domestic cattle, now extinct.

Jason: a Greek mythological hero, famous for his quest of the Golden Fleece.

Cahòw: a bird indigenous to Bermuda.

Origins

In this poem Wingfield contemplates what she knows of her own ancestry, working backwards from the migration of her forebears through the 'pedlar, diplomat, landlord, peasant' of the seventeenth and eighteenth centuries, towards pre-history.

While Satyrs Hunted for a Nymph

Satyrs: demigods, represented as men but with the legs and feet of a goat, horned heads and thick body hair.

Nymphs: female deities.

lymph: a colourless alkaline fluid, derived from various tissues and organs of the body, resembling blood but containing no red corpuscles.

Even So

Lean-legged John: John the Baptist, who fasted in the wilderness for forty days and forty nights.

Poisoned in Search of the Medicine of Immortality

Hsüang Tsung was Emperor of China (712-756). He was the longest reigning of all the T'ang monarchs, restoring China to good government, peace and prosperity. His reign ended in tragedy, however, largely as a result of his own actions and policies.

Epiphany in a Country Church

sanfoin: a high-yield silage or hay crop.

Ease

Rhadamanthus: a wise king, the Son of Zeus and Europa.

In Greek mythology the *Elysian Fields* were where the souls of the heroic and virtuous went after death.

A Tuscan Farmer

Hercules: the son of Zeus and the mortal Alcmene. He was known for his physical strength and heroic exploits.

hydra: the many-headed serpent in Greek mythology.

hell-dog: supernatural dogs are common in folklore – the most common of these is Cerberus from Greek mythology.

Janus

In the mythology of ancient Rome, *Janus* is the god of beginnings and endings, and also of transitions – hence his association with doors, gateways and portals. He is usually depicted with two faces, one looking to the future and the other the past. The Romans dedicated the month of January to Janus.

Part 1
shuttlecock and battledore: an early game, the precursor of modern badminton.

Darkness

stuffs: material for garments, textile fabric.

cassock: a long, close-fitting frock or tunic worn by Anglican clergymen.

mortar-board: a close-fitting cap surmounted by a stiffened square of similar material with a tassel; worn as an article of formal academic dress.

Carthage was destroyed by the Romans in 146 BC and re-founded to become one of the three most important cities of the empire.

'Written before Powerscourt, which had an adjacent burial ground for the family, was accidentally destroyed by fire in 1974.' [original note]

Cartography

Part 2
proconsul: originally a term used to describe the governor of a Roman province; in modern times it denotes a man placed in charge of colonial territory.

carronade: a short cast iron cannon in use from the 1770s to the 1850s.

Part 3
Cythera: a Greek island, strategically located opposite the south-eastern tip of the Peloponnese peninsula.

For My Dead Friends

Part 1
Parthenon: a temple on the Athenian Acropolis. It is the most important surviving building of Classical Greece and its sculptures are considered among the high points of Greek art.

Part 3
The most famous version of *Phaethon*'s story is found in Ovid's *Metamorphoses*. In order to affirm that his father is the sun god Helios, Phaethon is permitted to drive Helios's chariot. His failure to control it leads Zeus to kill him with a thunderbolt in order to prevent further disaster.

Opinion is divided on whether *Achilles* and *Patroclus* were lovers or comrades only. Achilles was distraught at the death of Patroclus, and the emotions he experienced while preparing for the young man's funeral power show him as a grieving and vulnerable man.

Part 4
that shell/now flushed by haze: traditionally conch shells, when held to the ear, resonate with the sound of the ocean. These shells are greyish-pink, a similar colour to the asphodel.

A Query

This poem seems to depict the taking of Constantinople by the Turks in 1453. The dome of Hagia Sophia, the principle cathedral of the city, depicted *Christ Pantokrator* (Almighty) with the Emperor Constantine IX and his wife. Though the mosaic in Hagia Sophia does not conflate the figures of emperor and Christ, other representations do so.

The Leaves Darken

Book 4 of *The Odyssey* provides an account of *Menelaus* on his return home from Troy. His ship was blown off course and he was stranded in *Egypt*. He later experienced misgivings for the human cost of the Trojan War.

Village Seasons

keys: the winged seeds of the ash tree.

Sonnet (II)

Alexander the Great's corpse was placed in a gold sarcophagus and, in turn, in a gold casket, after death.

King *Arthur* reputedly died after a wound to his head.

Phaedra was the daughter of Minos and Pasiphae, sister of Ariadne and wife of Theseus. She fell in love with Hippolytus, the son of Theseus born either by Hippolyta, queen of the Amazons, or Antiope, her sister.

Artemis: daughter of Zeus and Leto; she was the Hellenic goddess of the hunt, wilderness and wild animals.

Or Mons, or Troy, or mound of Jericho: cities made famous by classical and Biblical history. Both Troy and Jericho are also important for their legendary status.

An Answer from Delphi

Part 2
Wingfield considers the different systems of belief that have shaped the search for meaning, from the early Christian rituals – with gold mosaic and plainchant – to German settlers in Britain of the fifth and sixth centuries.

when a conch shell brays: 'As was once the custom when Bermudian fishermen came ashore with their catch.' [original note]

Part 3

Parnassos: Mount Parnassus in Greece.

No Castalian words: Castalia was a nymph transformed by Apollo into a fountain at Delphi. She had the power to inspire poetry in those who drank from, or listened to, her waters.

Not Forgetting Aeneas Sylvius

Pope Pius II was born *Aeneas Silvius* Bartholomeus (1405-1464).

Tyranny

Antigone was the daughter of the incestuous union between Oedipus, King of Thebes, and Jocasta, Oedipus's mother. After the king's death, Antigone's two brothers – Eteocles and Polynices – were meant to reign over Thebes in turn. Eteocles' refusal to share power caused a violent conflict in which both brothers were killed. Creon, King of Corinth, declared that – though Eteocles could be buried appropriately Polynices should be left outside the city to be devoured by animals. Antigone claimed this was against the law of the gods and buried Polynices herself, thus provoking Creon's anger.

Teiresias: the blind prophet of Thebes, famous for having lived as a woman for seven years.

Carpaccio

Vittore *Carpaccio* (1465-1525/6) was an Italian painter of the Venetian school. Among the most famous of his works is the cycle of nine paintings called 'The Legend of Saint Ursula'.

St Ursula: a fourth-century Romano-British princess who, prior to her political marriage to a pagan governor, undertook a European pilgrimage. She travelled with 11,000 virgin handmaidens to Rome, and then to Cologne, which was being besieged by Huns. All the virgins were beheaded.

Brigid

Brigid was the daughter of the Dagda and one of the Tuatha Dé Danann. Later her characteristics were merged with those of her Christian counterpart, St Brigid of Kildare.

One's Due

Ge-Hinnom: a valley to the south and south-west of Jerusalem, traditionally a place of burning and punishment. Synonymous with hell or purgatory.

Remote Matters

Dunwich: a village in Suffolk, England. Severe coastal erosion since the thirteenth century has caused the harbour and most of the town to disappear.

No Instructions

Dr John *Dee* (1527-1608/9) was a mathematician, astronomer and navigator. A consultant to Queen Elizabeth I, his intellectual interests combined science and magic. Though he believed that mathematics would provide the answer to the mystery of creation he also thought that understanding could be reached by summoning angels.

quasar: a compact region surrounding a large galaxy's central black hole.